Exploring
The Lower Walkham Valley

By PAUL RENDELL

FOREST PUBLISHING

First published in 1996 by FOREST PUBLISHING, Woodstock,
Liverton, Newton Abbot, Devon TQ12 6JJ

British Library Cataloguing in Publication Data

A catalogue record for this book is available from the British Library.

ISBN 0-9527297-1-7

Forest Publishing

Editorial, design and layout by:
Mike Lang

Typeset by:
Carnaby Typesetting, Torquay, Devon TQ1 1EG

Printed and bound in Great Britain by:
R. Mann, Newton Abbot, Devon.

Cover Photographs:

Top   –   The West Sortridge Consols Mine (also known as Gem
           Mine) below the Walkham (or Grenofen) Viaduct. c.1886.
                                    Capt. H. P. Chichester-Clark

Lower –   Grenofen Bridge.
                         Author's Collection

CONTENTS

ACKNOWLEDGEMENTS

I would like to thank the many people who have helped me with my research and to those who have checked the manuscript. I am especially indebted to Sandy Gerrard of Wembworthy for his interest and kindness in supplying me with specific information concerning the mines and minerals.

Kath Brewer, Torquay; Margaret Chichester-Clark, Whitchurch; Michael Cranmer (Western Morning News); Helen Harris, Whitchurch; Margaret Hicks, Grenofen House; Anthony R. Kingdom, Newton Ferrers; Karen Lang, Liverton; Peter Laxton, Grenofen; Peter Hamilton-Leggett, Walkhampton; Peggy Oxenford, Buckland Monachorum; Jon Turner (West Devon Borough Council); Adrienne Yelland, Liskeard; Robert Zaple, Newton Abbot.
Last, but not least, the staff of Plymouth Local Studies Library and also the staff at West Devon Record Office, including Paul Brough, John Fell, Anne Morgan and Emma West.

(Photographs are acknowledged individually in most instances)

DEDICATION

This book is dedicated to my mother, Ruth, and to my father, Derek, who helped me to appreciate the valley of the River Walkham from a very early age.

INTRODUCTION

The River Walkham trickles into life at a spot high up on northern Dartmoor known as Walkham Head, some 1,760 feet (530 metres) above sea level. Here, the overall scene is one of extreme bleakness, and the terrain is very boggy. Yet, it is also an area from which, for centuries, man has been able to draw on a rich source of peat for use in mines and as a fuel in the moorland dwellings.

From this somewhat inhospitable source, the river flows in a predominately southerly direction and may, loosely, be divided into three sections – the upper reaches being from Walkham Head to Merrivale Bridge, the middle reaches being from Merrivale Bridge to Bedford Bridge (also known locally as Magpie Bridge) and the lower reaches being from Bedford Bridge to Double Waters, where it becomes the main tributary of the River Tavy. In all, it extends to a length of approximately 10 miles and has numerous tributaries of its own, including Spriddle Lake, Dead Lake, Beckamoor Water, Pila Brook (also known as Long Ash Brook) and Yes Tor Brook.

The aim of this booklet is to help you explore the valley of the River Walkham below Bedford Bridge, which is situated on the main A386 road between Yelverton and Tavistock, just to the north-west of the village of Horrabridge. It is an area of outstanding natural beauty and one that is both rich in wildlife and industrial remains: it has been worked for copper, tin, arsenic and stone, bricks were made here from nearby clay and, until comparatively recent times, the railway line between Plymouth and Tavistock crossed the valley over two large viaducts.

In the pages that follow I have expanded on these facts and concluded with a description of a suggested circular walk, pointing out the many items of interest along the way. In doing so, I hope that I have achieved my aim of making your visit to this beautiful valley all the more worthwhile. I must, however, close on a word of warning. Old mines and quarries, whilst areas of great interest, are also places of considerable danger, so please take care and at all times remember the Country Code:

4

- Enjoy the countryside and respect its life and work
- Guard against all risk of fire
- Fasten all gates
- Keep your dogs under close control
- Keep to public paths across farmland
- Use gates and stiles to cross fences, hedges and walls
- Leave livestock, crops and machinery alone
- Take your litter home
- Help to keep all water clean
- Protect wildlife, plants and trees
- Take special care on country roads
- Make no unnecessary noise
- Respect private land

Paul Rendell
February 1996

A view of the Lower Walkham valley from Sticklepath Wood looking towards Whitchurch. To the left can be seen part of the Walkham, or Grenofen, Viaduct. c. 1950.
Western Morning News
(Courtesy of West Devon Record Office)

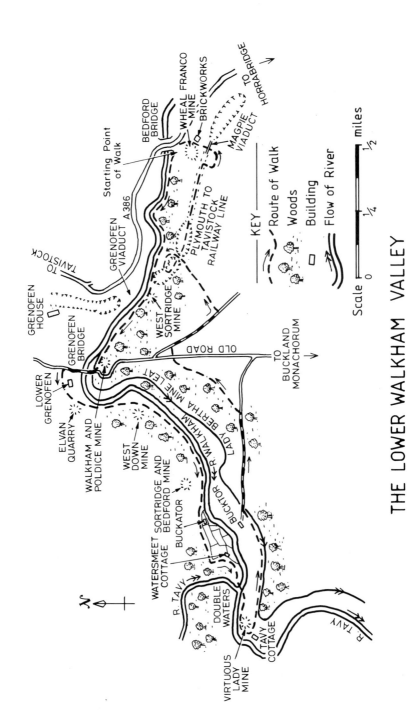

THE LOWER WALKHAM VALLEY

KEY

- - - Route of Walk

🌳 Woods

◻ Building

Flow of River

Scale

0   ¼   ½   miles

WHEAL FRANCO MINE

BRICKWORKS

TO HORRABRIDGE

MAGPIE VIADUCT

BEDFORD BRIDGE

Starting Point of Walk

A386

PLYMOUTH TO TAVISTOCK RAILWAY LINE

GRENOFEN VIADUCT

TO TAVISTOCK

WEST SORTRIDGE MINE

GRENOFEN HOUSE

GRENOFEN BRIDGE

OLD ROAD

TO BUCKLAND MONACHORUM

LOWER GRENOFEN

ELVAN QUARRY

WALKHAM AND POLDICE MINE

R. WALKHAM

LADY BERTHA MINE LEAT

WEST DOWN MINE

BUCKTOR

WATERSMEET SORTRIDGE AND BEDFORD MINE COTTAGE

BUCKATOR

N

R. TAVY

DOUBLE WATERS

TAVY COTTAGE

R. TAVY

VIRTUOUS LADY MINE

6

I

THE MINES

Economically, the most important mineral mined in the area both surrounding and including the Lower Walkham valley was copper, which was obtained almost exclusively by deep mining operations. Several of the mines had earlier beginnings, but with advances in mining technology and engineering (including the introduction of the steam engine) greater depths were attainable with the result that by the 18th and 19th centuries previously inaccessible lodes were being extracted. Many mines also produced tin, lead and arsenic as by-products, and those that could diversified as fluctuations occurred through time in natural availability and mineral market prices. Therefore, when discussing subterranean activity, it must be remembered that many of the mines underwent fluidity in mineral output.

In most instances the actual technique for removing any of the ores was largely consistent. Depending upon the deposition and depth of the ore-bearing veins, or lodes, shafts (usually vertical) were sunk into the ground and adits, or levels, worked along the mineral veins in a more horizontal manner. Frequently adits were dual purpose since they could facilitate access to the mineral face as well as act as a means of draining a mine. Should the minerals continue beneath the level of a drainage adit, then water would have to be pumped up to this level before its expulsion from the mine. This was achieved in a variety of ways, dependent upon the available technology, economic constraints and the quantity of water involved. They ranged from hand-powered, horse-powered or, ironically, water-powered pumps relying on waterwheels for operational purposes to the most efficient mechanical steam-driven pumps, which could facilitate access to greater depths since the water could be more effectively removed.

The ore was mined using levels, which were generally positioned at the depth where vertical shafts intercepted the mineral lodes: it was removed from both the roof and the floor of the level, a system known as 'stoping'. Depending upon the location of the lode, these could extend either upwards (overhand) or downwards (underhand), and in the larger mines substantial underground cavities were created. This technique, incidentally, had developed from surface working, where opencast quarries known as openworks, or beams, removed the mineral-bearing rock in a downwards movement, thus

7

producing the distinctive trenches which survive in the countryside throughout the mineral-rich areas.

In order to bring the ore from below adit level to the surface, it had to be winched. The earliest windlasses were hand-powered; these were later replaced by horse-driven whims or water-powered winches until, ultimately, steam power enabled far greater depths to be reached. Often the ore was conveyed up a series of smaller shafts, or winzes, from level to level until it reached the surface. In this instance the ore was carried in wheelbarrows or, as in the case of some mines, in horse-drawn wagons that ran along rails. These smaller shafts were also useful in another respect. Together with the larger shafts and, of course, the adits, they created a certain amount of ventilation for the deeper workings, a process that was aided in some instances by bellows or fans. Even so, ventilation was notoriously bad in mines and this, added to inevitably damp and dusty conditions, was a major cause of health problems amongst the miners.

At the rock-face the ore was removed in a variety of ways. 'Plug and feathering' was one of the earliest whereby a conical rod was driven between metal wedges into a cracked or drilled hole, causing the rock to split. 'Fire setting' was another alternative used to achieve the same effect. In this instance the rock was heated before being cooled rapidly by dousing it with water. However, this particular method was rather slow and unhealthy as the levels would fill with smoke and become impossible to work for some time. Later, by the 17th century, metal tools had been developed sufficiently as to enable rocks to be drilled and holes to be bored, thereby allowing the process to be speeded up somewhat. Some mines also went on to develop this method for charges of gunpowder, which were lit using tapers of quills or straw. Needless to say, firing gunpowder in this manner was extremely dangerous, and it was just as well that safety fuses were soon invented. Later still, with the development of high explosives, the boring of shotholes was to become an important aspect of mining technology.

Depending upon the type of mineral which was being extracted, different methods needed to be employed at the mine surface in order to separate the ore from its surrounding material (gangue) so that the metal could be obtained. Although the exact nature of the process varied according to the mineral, the basic principles were crushing, using stamps or rollers, followed by washing, sorting, roasting or calcining, in some instances, and smelting. The crushing, washing and sorting procedures were generally carried out very close to the mine, as was the roasting and calcining, but the smelting was generally carried out at a distant specialist centre where the material from a number of mines was processed together. Arsenic required special attention since to arrive at a purer product the vapours produced after the arsenic was crushed, washed and roasted would pass through flues and condense on the walls as a white powdery residue. It was also lethal, and those employed to scrape it off were clothed with nostrils and mouths padded, ears blocked and hands and feet specially covered. Nevertheless, from the 1860s, with the decline of the copper industry, arsenic assumed greater importance to some of the mines in the Lower Walkham valley and was used for a wide variety of purposes, including paint dyes, glass, weedkillers, insecticides and medicines.

Within the Lower Walkham valley there were at least six discreet mines. Bearing in mind the often confused nature of underground workings, with lodes undoubtedly merging, it is, however, difficult (if not impossible) to define precisely the extent of each mine. Moreover, the picture is further complicated by mergers of different companies and name changes. Nevertheless, for identification purposes, the major mines known to have existed are indicated on the map appearing on page 6 and some specific details concerning each of them are set out below, although it has to be said that any observation of surface remains bears an uncanny resemblance to the study of an iceberg: the observer may see the remains of buildings, dumps and shafts, but the vast majority is hidden from view in a complex network of subterranean workings!

Wheal Franco (SX 509701) –   also known as Wheal Robert, or Wheal Sir Massey, and Franco Consols.

This was one of the most important copper mines in the district. It opened in 1823 under the control of William Patey of Plymouth (a shopkeeper), John Paull of Tavistock (a miner) and John Boswarva of Plymouth (an accountant), and initially worked the lodes to the west of what is now the A386 Plymouth to Tavistock road, near Bedford Bridge. In 1840, however, some two years after the main shaft had reached 160 fathoms, and the workforce had grown to over 130, a new shaft was sunk on the other side of the road, and it was the result of this that the mine became so productive. In 1846, for example, some 140 tons of copper ore were raised every month.

Over the ensuing years a further six shafts were sunk and, by 1862, a total of 10,333 tons of 10% copper ore had been sold for £51,500, making it one of the most productive mines in Devon. Thereafter, production appears to have gone into decline and, in 1870, a new company called Wheal Franco Consols took over after acquiring the land between the 'old' and the 'new' Franco workings, which contained three lodes of black and grey copper ore. Suttons Shaft was sunk in May of that year and drained by means of an adit (to a depth of 23 fathoms) as well as by at least six waterwheels of varying sizes, all of which were driven by water from the Grimstone and Sortridge Leat. Unfortunately, though, the mine had always suffered from drainage problems, and in the spring of 1871 it experienced considerable flooding. By this time the workforce had already dwindled to ten and only around 70 tons of copper ore had been raised, valued at just over £100. Moreover, steadily falling production of ore led to the mine becoming unprofitable and the final returns in 1873 showed that only 45 tons of ore producing 2.8 tons of metal (worth £163. 10s.) had been raised. Nevertheless, it was not until around 1875 that the mine was finally abandoned, following a brief period during which the old dumps were reworked.

Part of the Wheal Franco Mine workings below Magpie Viaduct. c. 1918.

Author's Collection

West Sortridge Consols (SX 495705) – also known as (Little) Gem or Walkham Valley Mine.

This mine was reopened in the early 1850s for the exploitation of copper, but actually went on to produce rather more in the way of tin and arsenic during its lifetime. Two lodes were worked on the north-eastern slopes of the valley by Lucy's Shaft (ESE of Grenofen Bridge), with one shallow adit and one deep adit, and also on the other side of the River Walkham, the lodes trending approximately east to west to a width of up to 4 feet and continuing some 10 to 15 fathoms below the river. Lucy's Shaft was vertical and met the northern lode at 20 fathoms, although it was reputed that the mine captain closed this section in the hope of opening it again at some later date – to his own advantage! However, this type of yarn was common in nearly all mining communities and reflected the mistrust felt by many working miners towards their management, so its authenticity cannot be guaranteed! Whatever, it would seem that the mine's most profitable period was between 1871 and

1874, when it produced 31 tons of black tin valued at £2,483. 10s., and it is known that the quest for tin continued there between 1883 and 1902.

Surface remains still visible to this day include those of the workshops, three circular pits (called buddles) in which tin was concentrated, a stamp-bed that had originally housed a set of four water-powered Cornish stamps for crushing the ore and the wheelpit in which the wheel that provided the power for the dressing process had rotated. The calciner (roasting oven), on the other hand, is now completely ruinous, although some other related buildings do survive on the opposite side of the river, albeit privately-owned. It should also be mentioned that Gem Cottage (SX 49427080) was originally the Count House for the mine; it was here that the ore was weighed in the presence of a bailiff, who took dues of 1 shilling for every ton of ore that he saw weighed.

Walkham and Poldice (SX 491708) – also known as Old Poldice, Devon Poldice or Walkhampton United.

This mine is believed to have been on the site of an earlier tinwork called Poldice and recorded in 1717, and may well have had even earlier origins. It was situated on the south side of the River Walkham near the headweir of the Lady Bertha Mine Leat and commenced operations in 1865. The workings, however, were not extensive – the shafts and adits were shallow and some of the lodes were worked from the surface by openworks – and only comparatively small yields of tin, lead and copper were obtained. Between 1865 and 1866, for example, the returns show that 4.9 tons of lead ore, 25 tons of copper ore and 1.1 tons of tin ore were brought to the surface. The mine eventually closed in 1890 and nowadays the wheelpit and remains of some walls in the vicinity are about the only evidence that it ever existed, although further up the hillside there is also a tip of rubble and an adit, which leads into the shaft.

A view of Walkham and Poldice Mine, near Grenofen Bridge, showing the stamps and waterwheel.

Capt. H. P. Chichester-Clark

West Down Mine (SX 488706)

This mine may never have been very large, and in its later life was probably no more than an unsuccessful prospecting operation.

A vertical shaft was driven on the northern bank of the River Walkham near Grenofen Bridge, with an adit about 80 yards away in a south-westerly direction, and a line of prospecting or trial pits were sunk towards the shaft of Sortridge and Bedford Mine, the latter with the apparent aim of locating the copper lodes running from that particular mine. These pits date from 1864 to 1865 and can be seen from the bottom of the trackway descending West Down to Grenofen Bridge, where there is also situated a well-preserved chimney stack. That the pits are still there suggests that they were unsuccessful, and the apparent lack of any records of production levels only serves to uphold the view that this applied to the mine as a whole. However, it is known that the chief agent of the mine was called Thomas Neill and, similarly, that the mine secretary was called George Down. Other relics, meanwhile, include a second chimney stack located much higher up the hillside, below a rock outcrop. It is partly ruinous, has a square base and stands about 8 feet high: according to local knowledge, it was built to overcome air pollution problems in the valley caused by arsenic fumes being emitted from the chimney stack situated lower down the hillside and must, therefore, be of later date. The flue can be followed from the remains of the buildings at the bottom of the valley to the base of the chimney.

Incidentally, a pig of metal, now housed in Plymouth Museum, was once found in the entrance to an adit at the foot of West Down. It weighs just over 4 kilograms and measures 14.4cm by 14.4cm by 1.6cm. On the lower surface the symbol IIL is etched, and the upper surface has an incised sign, together with six partial impressions of a George I sixpenny piece. It has been described as a pig of lead, although there has been some debate and others have suggested that it may be silver or tin. Whatever its composition, its discovery in the vicinity of this mine certainly suggests mining activity hereabouts during the early part of the 18th century.

Sortridge and Bedford Mine (SX 482703)

This was a small operation linked with that of West Down Mine. A shaft near the centre of the Down was sunk to 46 fathoms, with a level at 20 fathoms, and two adits were driven, one on the eastern bank of the River Tavy, which proved to be barren, and the other on the northern bank of the River Walkham. There is also a small pit to the south-west of the site, but the most likely implication is that this mine reflects a largely unsuccessful prospecting operation. The shaft has long since been filled, but the remains of a dump still exist.

Virtuous Lady Mine (SX 474698)

This mine, situated close to the confluence of the Walkham and Tavy rivers, at Double Waters, was worked as early as the reign of Elizabeth I, after whom it was reputedly named. Thereafter, exploitation was somewhat sporadic, and this was a pattern that was to continue after it was known to have reopened in 1816 as a copper mine. Nevertheless, it contained several rich ore pockets, and at least five shafts are known; there were probably more. The underground workings, in fact, continued to the opposite side of the River Tavy, the deepest being some 20 fathoms below the river.

The mine's most productive periods appear to have been around the mid-1850s, and again, albeit to a lesser extent, between the years 1870 to 1872, when 284 tons of copper ore worth £1,829. 16s. and 6.3 tons of tin ore worth £718. 6s. were raised. The ore, itself, was taken by packhorses (led by young boys) across a bridge over the River Tavy and up to Orestocks on the Tavistock to Bere Alston road. From here it was subsequently taken to Morwellham in a train of horse-drawn wagons and then shipped to South Wales, where it was smelted.

Virtuous Lady Mine and the River Tavy.

Author's Collection

Power for the mine was obtained by means of a number of waterwheels, which were fed through a system of leats taken off the River Walkham and supplemented, in some instances, by water draining off springs on the hillside.

13

VIRTUOUS LADY MINE

Of these, the main leat was Lady Bertha, which also served the mine from which it took its name lower down the valley of the River Tavy. From 1850 the mine was also worked by steam power, but the steam engines were expensive and, unfortunately, their arrival coincided with a reduction in the price of copper. Indeed, during its later life the mine was forced to diversify into other minerals, including tin and arsenic reworked from earlier dumps. Furthermore, severe financial problems eventually arose and, by April 10th 1873, Virtuous and Bedford Mine (its current name) had gone into liquidation.

Today, substantial surface remains survive of this once thriving mine, although many are located on privately-owned land. There are the remains of dumps, an engine-house, wheelpits, leats, shafts and other buildings, one of which housed the crushing rolls (these were driven by a waterwheel, the same one that was used in conjunction with the pumping of a shaft on the opposite side of the river by means of a system of flat rods). The former mine captain's house can also still be seen, having for many years now been used as a private residence, while up until the early 1970s it was possible to be taken around the underground caverns where, apart from the remains of the workings, substantial amounts of various crystallised minerals could be seen. Towards the end of the 19th century, in fact, the underground remains were an extremely popular attraction to visitors.

The mine captain's house, situated high above the River Tavy at Virtuous Lady Mine.
Author's Collection

15

Although situated beyond the area of the Lower Walkham valley, there were also several other mines or mining related ventures in the locality that deserve a passing mention. One of the more profitable was **Sortridge Consols** (SX 510708), which was earlier known as West Wheal Robert and thus connected with Wheal Franco, and which was reopened in 1854. Here, a rich deposit of copper was found 5 feet below the surface, and it was reported that within just a few months of the mine reopening some £3,200 worth of copper had been sold at an outlay to the company of some £600. By then the workings had reached a maximum depth of 30 fathoms. At the 40 fathom level, however, output began to decline and, in 1855, a new shaft was sunk using a more powerful engine. But again, with increasing depth, the returns became poorer. As a result the mine eventually closed, only to be reopened in 1883 and worked sporadically until 1902: this was in spite of an accident occurring in 1883 in which the mine captain and another man were both drowned. In 1924 the dumps were worked briefly for arsenic, and it is said that during World War II some of the material from the slag dumps were used in the construction of Harrowbeer airfield at Yelverton.

Tavy Consols (SX 469688) was another productive mine, which was worked between 1852 and 1891 for the extraction of copper, tin and arsenic. It has been reported that the lodes were particularly rich in arsenical ore and that at one time the calciners on the mine were commonly 'burning' 125 tons each month, resulting in a monthly output of 15 tons of refined arsenic. Nearby, arsenic was also known to have been produced at **Little Duke,** which was a venture owned by the Duke of Bedford.

Also located nearby, but on the opposite side of the River Tavy, were the copper mines owned by the Lady Bertha United Mining Company Limited known as **Lady Bertha** (SX 471689), **South Lady Bertha** (SX 477682) and **East Lady Bertha** (SX 478690). Although production levels for East and South Lady Bertha appear to be unknown, Lady Bertha produced 4,384 tons of copper ore and 1,682 tons of arsenic between 1855 and 1882.

Other, less significant, mines included **North Roborough Down Mine** (SX 513684), **Wheal Rose** (SX 522697) – often known as Walkhampton Consols and where there are still surface remains as well as those of a wheelpit and part of a leat – and also **Furzehill Mine** (SX 515692). However, this latter mine, also called Furzehill Wood Mine, is probably better known for the disaster that occurred there in 1866 when seven miners and a boy were all drowned after some old flooded workings had inadvertently been tapped. A contemporary account of the tragedy appeared in the *Western Morning News.*

In concluding this chapter, mention must be made of the miners and, in particular, the harsh and hazardous working conditions that they had to endure. There were obvious dangers from roof falls, explosives, toxic and noxious gases, and mines were nearly always susceptible to flooding, especially at depth. Indeed, it is a sad fact that many miners perished as a result of drowning, either through mechanical failure or, as occurred at Furzehill Mine, through accidental opening of abandoned flooded workings.

Conditions at best were cramped and dirty. Polluted water and unsanitary conditions below ground caused many viral diseases; in addition, there were obviously impacts and lesions that could become dangerously infected. Sight defects, caused by prolonged exposure to inadequate lighting coupled with dusty atmospheres, were another common complaint. Although candles were used, economy was the key, since the miners were expected to provide their own. Respiratory conditions were also encountered, since working at depth results in heat and humidity within the air being greater. On rising to the surface, a blast of cold air to the lungs was often a cause for bronchial complaints. In addition, the extractive process produced dust which, in a confined space, was readily inhaled and could cause several other breathing disorders. Many miners fell to their deaths at the end of a day, losing their footing on ladders as they climbed to the surface. It is hardly surprising, therefore, that many miners never reached the age of 40, especially since some had begun to work in the mine by the time that they were eight years old.

Horrabridge, home to some of the miners working in the Lower Walkham valley. c. 1912.

Author's Collection

Of course, a gruelling 10–12 hour day was only part of the story. Many faced long walks home to places such as Tavistock, Buckland Monachorum and Whitchurch. Then there were daily duties at home to be completed before bed and another early morning walk back to the Walkham valley the following day. Some miners did choose to stay in Horrabridge during the week, and at Wheal Franco Mine temporary housing was provided. They would bring their own provisions and, if time permitted, would cook a meal in the evenings.

Depending upon the nature of his employment, the miner could receive either wages and provide his own tools and equipment – a Tutworker – or, under the Tribute System, he would receive a percentage of the total value of ores produced, less the costs of tools and other materials. Under this system every miner kept a close eye upon fluctuations in the mineral market and dreamed of striking a particularly rich lode!

Naturally, not all of those who worked at the mines were miners; a number worked on the surface processing the ores. Some of the mines in the Lower Walkham valley still have remains of the processing floors where these surface workers carried out the skilful tasks associated with separating the minerals from their associated wastes, or gangue. Most of the surviving processing sites belong to the 19th century, but an interesting example of an earlier site lies just outside the Lower Walkham valley at SX 514695 and is known as the Little Horrabridge Blowing House. Here tin was being crushed and smelted during the 16th century and, although the actual building no longer survives, archaeological excavation produced many stone artefacts. These included mortar stones, crazing stones and mouldstones, all used in the process of crushing and smelting tin and now preserved.

II

LESSER INDUSTRIES

Whilst mining was undoubtedly the most important industry in the valley, there were a number of lesser industries carried out over the years. These included elvan quarrying, the manufacture of bricks and various milling operations:-

Elvan Quarrying

Elvan quarrying took place during the 19th century to the west of Grenofen Bridge at SX 488708, where the remains of the quarry are still visible. The stone was used as roadstone and as ornamental carving for buildings and monuments, and has an unusual and commercially useful characteristic in that it is soft to extract, but hardens upon contact with the air. It does, however, have a very limited distribution, occurring only in Devon and Cornwall: its formation seems to be linked to those geological processes that produced the metallic mineral-bearing ores in these areas.

Brick Manufacture

For a number of years up until the end of the 19th century there was a brickworks situated between Bedford Bridge and Magpie Viaduct, at SX 504703, which utilised local clay deposits. Unfortunately, little now remains to show that it ever existed, but there are bricks within the area that bear the *Horrabridge* brand mark.

Milling

As far as it is known, the only mill actually within the confines of the valley not involved with the processing of ore was situated at SX 499705. This was Magpie Mill where, in the 1880s, violin strings were produced. The mill, locally referred to as the old gut mill, also produced sausages.

It is worth mentioning, however, that there were a number of other mills in the locality such as Phoenix Mill (SX 514694), which was used for a very wide range of milling operations that included corn, fulling, leather, paper and wool.

✳✳✳✳✳

III

THE RAILWAY VIADUCTS

There were once two large railway viaducts to be seen in the valley, one of which, Magpie Viaduct, is still in evidence to this day, albeit now in a somewhat dangerous state of repair. Built of blue Staffordshire brick, it is 216 yards long and stands at a maximum height of 62 feet over a small tributary of the River Walkham, just to the south of Bedford Bridge. It was first brought into use in 1902 as a replacement of an earlier timber structure with stone piers; this had been designed by Isambard Kingdom Brunel in conjunction with the construction of the railway line between Plymouth and Tavistock by the South Devon & Tavistock Railway Company during the years 1856 to 1859.

Although no longer in existence, the larger viaduct was that which carried the same railway line across the River Walkham. This, too, had originally been a timber structure, and was once described as 'the most matured design of Brunel's timber viaducts'. Comprising 15 spans, each of 66 feet, and two end spans measuring almost 60 feet each, it was 367 yards long and 132 feet high, and was not only beautiful to behold, but fitted gracefully into the landscape. The timber used came from the Baltic, was kyanised as a precaution against fire and had an average lifespan of 30 years.

The more recent structure was completed in 1910. This retained the then existing masonry piers, only raised in brickwork to take the bedstones (each weighing 6 tons), which, in turn, were lowered into position from a temporary gantry erected at the floor level of the viaduct. The reconstruction work also entailed the main girders being placed into position on to the bedstones by two 12-ton cranes (one at either end), cross-girders being threaded in externally by 3-ton cranes, and the rail-bearers being lowered on to the cross-girders from above by removing portions of the decking, which, itself, was subsequently replaced by steel flooring for the permanent way.

Sadly, as already mentioned, this famous landmark has now gone, as, indeed, has the impressive sight of a steam train making its way across the valley. The railway line closed at the end of 1962 – in rather bizarre circumstances as the last scheduled trains failed to run because of heavy snow (this was to mark the beginning of the worst winter conditions seen since 1891 and

1947) – and in 1964, once track lifting had been completed, Walkham Viaduct (also frequently referred to as Grenofen Viaduct) was partly dismantled before being demolished during the following year.

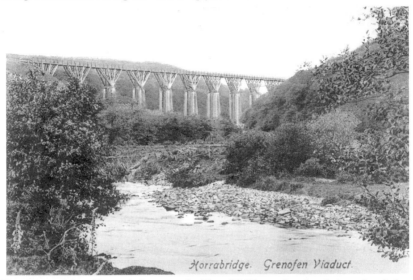

Two views of the railway viaduct over the River Walkham, showing the massive timber superstructure (above) replaced with steel (below).

Author's Collection

✳✳✳✳✳

IV

GRENOFEN MANOR

The name Grenofen goes back at least as far as 1238, although it was then recorded as Grenefenne, meaning 'at the green marsh'. The house with this name almost certainly originated as a farmstead and, together with the surrounding land, was owned for centuries by the Pollard family of Treleigh near Redruth in Cornwall. Only in the early part of the 18th century was there a change of ownership when it came within the possession of the Knighton family, who proceeded to extensively alter the property. Later, when he married into the Knighton family in 1810, the estate passed to George Drake and, again, extensive alterations followed that included the construction of the present bow-windowed frontage.

Grenofen House. c. 1940.

Western Morning News
(Courtesy of West Devon Record Office)

In 1830 the house was purchased at a public auction by the Rev. Jonathan Philips Carpenter from Mount Tavy, Tavistock. He added the drawing room and, interestingly, some of its original wallpaper was discovered in 1956, a sample being sent to the Victoria and Albert Museum. After his death in 1843, the house was let to the Morris family, who were deeply involved with local mining activity in the area and who were also related to the famous poet, artist and philosopher, William Morris.

In 1853 Harriett Carpenter married William Henry Chichester, of Arlington Court, Barnstaple. They then took possession of Grenofen House and were responsible for many garden improvements which, together with the interest that William Chichester had in glass, china and pictures, helped to make Grenofen House a typical example of a well-off Victorian gentleman's country residence.

The estate remained in the Chichester family until 1956, when it was sold to Cyril R. Smythe and became used for commercial purposes that included the manufacture of plastic products. By 1979, however, the house was almost derelict, and had to be rebuilt prior to being used as a country club: a new wing was added in 1983. More recently, in 1987, it was converted into residential apartments.

A gathering at Grenofen House in 1894.

Capt. H. P. Chichester-Clark

✳✳✳✳✳

23

V

FLORA AND FAUNA

The valley contains a rich and varied range of flora and fauna due to the different habitats, which include woodland, moorland, streams and the river. Below is just a small selection:–

The Common Tormentil, which is also frequently found on Dartmoor, thrives in the drier peaty acidic areas, particularly where the turf is short, and grows from a woody rootstock. Its slender stems bear pretty little yellow flowers from mid to late summer, and the tannin contained in its roots has astringent properties.

The Heath Spotted Orchis also thrives in acidic soils and may be seen in places as diverse as heath, moorlands and damp, marshy areas beside rivers. That the damp, wooded valley of the River Walkham is ideally suited to it is clearly evident as, indeed, it is in the Erme Valley, near Ivybridge. It is usually between 15 and 30 centimetres high and its flowers, which appear between early June and August, vary from light pink to lilac-rose with a pattern of reddish dots.

Gorse or, as it is more commonly known locally, furze is a large shrub that grows up to about 3 metres high, usually in large masses in rough grassy locations. Its flowering period is normally between March and July, but because there are other, smaller, types of gorse that are in flower at different times of the year there is a local saying 'when gorse is not flowering, kissing is out of fashion'. Although extremely prickly, gorse is sometimes used as a winter feed for cattle, the spines being thoroughly crushed beforehand, and at one time was also known to have been used as a fuel.

Lichens are common throughout the valley, and in the middle reaches of the River Walkham, near Merrivale, is a nature reserve which was designated so because of the rich and rare lichens in the vicinity. If lichens are seen growing on trees it is a sign of pure air. On West Down, and above Sticklepath Wood, sometimes 'Pixie's Matchsticks' (*Cladonia Floerkeana*) can be seen. These are grey branches with red 'matchstick' ends and grow to some 2 or 3 centimetres.

Bracken is the commonest fern in the valley, as it is on Dartmoor, and it, too, thrives in acidic soils. It can cover large areas but, unfortunately, kills off almost all the other vegetation of the ground that it occupies and is generally regarded as a pest. Despite this, it does have a lovely golden brown colour in the autumn and, in times past, served as bedding for animals after being cut by farmers. Nowadays this is seldom practised, although bracken is still cut within the valley for use as a mulch by a local garden centre.

The Elder is more frequently seen as a shrub, but it can grow to a tree as high as 10 metres and has often been referred to as a 'living medicine chest'. Its flowers, creamy yellow in colour, are used in tea and wine, and elderflower water is still sold as a mild skin cleanser. In addition, its berries, green initially, but deep purple by around August, are used for wine, chutney, jam and jellies, while the mature, hard wood is used for a whole variety of purposes, including the manufacture of small household articles and toys. Like many trees, Elder was supposed also to have magical powers.

The Pedunculate Oak is the more common of the two varieties of native deciduous oak, and this is particularly true in the valley and on Dartmoor. It immediately differs from the sessile oak by the acorns growing on long stalks called peduncles – hence its name – whereas the sessile acorns grow directly from the twigs. The leaves, too, are different as those of the pedunculate oak are pale green whilst those of the sessile oak are dark green and have shallower indentations. Apart from their important role in supporting a wealth of wildlife by playing host to birds, insects, mammals, fungi and lichens to name but a few, the oak trees (and other trees) in the valley would once also have been cut down and used in conjunction with the working of the mines.

Roe Deer love woods and plantations, and this valley has a good tree cover, particularly near Double Waters, where there is a large plantation. The **fox** is common on Dartmoor and can sometimes be seen above the tree line: it feeds on small vertebrates, insects, berries and fruit, and during the summer enjoys beetles and rabbits. **Badgers**, too, may be seen from time to time, though rarely during daylight, but the **grey squirrel** – introduced into the British Isles from North America in the 1870s and now classed as a pest because it strips the bark from trees – is a common sight.

Herons, dippers, grey wagtails and **kingfishers** can be seen on the river, and there are **salmon** and **brown trout** in it, while **kestrels, buzzards** and **ravens**, the largest of our crows, may be seen flying overhead. In the woods there are **nuthatches, tree creepers, green woodpeckers, great spotted woodpeckers, tawny owls, blackbirds, jays** and **magpies**, among many others.

Once **hares** and **woodcock** lived here as well, but they are no longer seen. Nevertheless, there is still a lot to see, so remember to be observant at all times whilst exploring the valley – it will certainly be worth it!

❄❄❄❄❄

VI

A SUGGESTED WALK

This walk is routed so as to include many of the items of interest in the Lower Walkham valley, which have already been mentioned in the preceding chapters. The ground can be muddy after heavy rain, but, otherwise, it is a fairly easy walk of about 5 miles. All river crossings are by bridges.

Starting Place: Bedford Bridge (also known locally as Magpie Bridge), which is situated on the main A386 road between Yelverton and Tavistock, just to the north-west of the village of Horrabridge (Map reference: SX 504704). It can be reached by private car or by public transport, using the bus service that runs between Plymouth and Tavistock. The bus service numbers are 83/84, and further information may be obtained by telephoning the Devonbus enquiry line on Exeter (01392) 382800 or on Plymouth (01752) 382800, or from the Tavistock Information Centre in Bedford Square – Telephone No: (01822) 612938.

Amenities: Toilets (normally closed during the winter) and public telephone at Bedford Bridge, plus shops, inns and a post office at the nearby village of Horrabridge.

Recommended Maps: The map on page 6 of this booklet is best used in conjunction with the Pathfinder Maps produced by the Ordnance Survey – Sheet 1349 (Bere Alston and Plymouth (North)) and Sheet 1340 (Tavistock).

Warning: As I have already mentioned in my Introduction, old mines and quarries are places of considerable danger, so please take care. This is particularly important as regards the underground workings, as many of the mines are unsafe.

Bedford Bridge, the starting place for the walk, was built in 1822 by the Trustees of the Plymouth and Tavistock Turnpike Trust as part of the system of turnpike roads from Plymouth to Tavistock. The toll to be paid at each Turnpike was as follows:

Waggon drawn by five or more horses	1/6d
Waggon/cart drawn by four horses	1/-
Waggon/cart drawn by two horses	9d
Waggon/cart drawn by one horse	6d
Coach/carriage drawn by six horses	1/-
Coach/carriage drawn by four horses	9d
Coach/carriage drawn by two horses	6d
Coach/carriage drawn by one horse	3d
Horse and rider	1d
Bullocks and other cattle	10d
Per score for sheep	5d

The toll-houses covering the immediate area were at Horrabridge and at Grenofen, which had the rather grand title of 'The Grenofen Gate Toll House'. However, the advent of the Plymouth to Tavistock Railway in 1859 resulted in a decline in the profits of the Plymouth and Tavistock Turnpike Trust and, in 1882, the toll-houses were sold, the one at Horrabridge currently being used as an antiques shop.

In 1850 there was also an inn near the bridge, under the proprietorship of a Mr. R. T. Newcombe and known as the King's Arms. This had almost certainly opened some time earlier to cater for the traffic on the then new turnpike road and, in all probability, closed at around the same time that the toll-houses ceased to exist, as is inferred by the renowned Dartmoor author, William Crossing. In his book entitled *The Western Gate of Dartmoor* (The Homeland Association, 1903) he states "… the Walkham is crossed at a place called Magpie, the name of an inn formerly existing here, but which has been closed for many years".

Bedford, or Magpie, Bridge over the River Walkham. The tall white building near the bridge was the King's Arms in 1850.

Author's Collection

It is now time to begin the walk. From the car park head towards the left bank of the river immediately below Bedford Bridge and follow the path downstream all the way to Grenofen Bridge.

This opening part of the walk will lead you past many relics of man's workings. One of the largest, yet the least obvious, is the viaduct that used to carry the railway line across the river. Demolished in 1965, its site can be recognised by a grassy ramp stretching steeply away from the river bank and, as if to bear witness to this once tall structure, there are a number of pieces of masonry protruding from the ground in the vicinity.

A little further on, and to the left, are the remains of a couple of ruinous buildings –used as workshops for the nearby West Sortridge Mine – while in the woods, and only a short distance away, is a fenced-off mine-shaft; this was the engine shaft to the mine. The path, however, continues to hug the river's edge and affords excellent opportunities for watching the fish darting around in the water. These include minnow and small brown trout.

Soon you will arrive at the take-off point of the Lady Bertha Mine Leat, easily identifiable by the sight of a ruined weir and wooden fish ladder. Lady Bertha Mine opened in 1855 and in the following year, after Mr. William Goss had obtained permission from Massey Lopes on 29th August, work commenced on constructing the leat and headweir to divert water from the river in order that it could be used to drive machinery at the mine. The leat, some 3 miles long with a fall of nearly 180 feet, was also used for Virtuous Lady Mine and remained in use until at least the 1950s, latterly supplying water to a cottage near Double Waters.

There is now a distinct bend in the river and, before you have walked much further, Grenofen Bridge will come into view. This ancient bridge, which existed well before 1675, as it was then reported as being in a state of disrepair, was a crossing place on the original road between Buckland Monachorum and Tavistock, both of which had abbeys in pre-dissolution days. Its 'modern day' equivalent has a single arch of 16 feet span and is 7 feet wide, and on a plan for the nearby mine many years ago was also named Sticklepath Bridge – not entirely inappropriate as 'stickle' means steep, which certainly applies to the hill leading down to it, and the adjoining wood is called Sticklepath Wood.

You now cross the bridge and walk a short distance up the hill before joining a bridleway going off to the left. This then leads you past Lower Grenofen Farm, through a gate and continues quite close to the river. After about 200 yards a high drystone wall will be reached. Behind this is the site of a 19th century elvan quarry, while a little further on, by taking the right-hand fork where the track diverges, you will pass a mine chimney and also several mining pits and hollows spread over a considerable area. This is the site of West Down Mine.

From this point, the path gradually leads down towards the river's edge once more, which you then follow for about a quarter of a mile. Thereafter the path begins to veer away from the river and leads you past what used to be a

Grenofen Bridge. The photograph shows a traction engine trying to cross the river in June 1893, the bridge being too small to accommodate it.

Capt. H. P. Chichester-Clark

Lower Grenofen Farm, which may have been built as a mine captain's house for Walkham and Poldice Mine.

Capt. H. P. Chichester-Clark

mine captain's house and is called Buckator. There is a wall here. Walk along-side it, uphill in the first instance on a rough concrete track, and then downhill by means of a small path as it drops sharply away towards the river. As you descend, there is a track joining the path from the right-hand side that was for-merly used by packhorses loaded with copper ore, while nearby, on the left-hand side, is seen Watersmeet Cottage, which was a former miner's dwelling.

Continue heading towards the river, then follow the path as it climbs away somewhat between two rock outcrops and walk through the gap. On doing so, you are immediately confronted by the sight of another river – the River Tavy, whose waters are united with those of the Walkham just a few yards to the left at a spot called Double Waters and which is well known for its wealth of river wildlife. The outcrop of rock here is not named, but the late Mrs. Bray of Tavistock, visiting in 1836, called the outcrop 'Goat Rock'. She also recalled how, a few years earlier, a poor girl walking to church had fallen off the wooden bridge across the River Walkham. She added that the old wooden bridge, known as a clam, had only one rail and mentioned that a farmer had also been found drowned down river from the bridge, it having been said that he had fallen off the wooden plank. Needless to say, the old bridge has long since gone and been replaced many times over the years.

The outcrop of rock at Double Waters referred to by Mrs Bray as 'Goat Rock'.
Author's Collection

Cross this wooden bridge and turn right along a track. You are now on the site of another copper mine, one of the largest in the surrounding area and called Virtuous Lady Mine. From here, follow the track up past Tavy Cottage (the last mine captain's dwelling), which is on the right-hand side, and also a garage. As the track turns right, beside the wall, there is a small path leading to a rock outcrop: follow this path around the rock outcrop until arriving at a dried-up leat. This is part of the Lady Bertha Mine Leat seen earlier and it is now to act as guide for the next section of the walk. A wall that appears on the left, incidentally, was part of an embankment which would allow water from the leat to flow along a wooden launder for the purposes of feeding a water-wheel lower down the valley.

A photograph taken between 1889 and 1892 showing the wooden launder used in conjunction with the Lady Bertha Mine Leat. Note the huge formation of icicles that has occurred due to serious leakage problems.

Peggy Oxenford

The leat should be followed until it disappears into a tunnel, but along the way take note of the stone bridge over it and the adjoining track, for this was another route used by packhorses laden with ore. A little further on, you will also see a small sluice gate, which was employed as part of a scheme to generate Hydro-electricity for use in the nearby houses.

On arriving at the spot where the leat disappears, turn left to join a roughly tarred road and then go off to the right. This road will lead you uphill, past a 'Public Bridleway' sign, through a wood and on to open moorland. However, just as you come out of the wood, turn off to the left on to a green track and follow this directly above the main tree line; it is rutted in places as farmers use it as a means of access when feeding their livestock.

Eventually, as you continue walking directly above the main tree line, another (smaller) green track will be seen going off to the right. Ignore this and, instead, carry straight on for a further 120 yards or so along the main track until it diverges. At this point, take the right-hand fork and within less than 50 yards you will reach another green track that goes off to the left and to the right. Again, this should be ignored as it is part of the original route between Buckland Monachorum and Tavistock mentioned earlier, and would take you off course.

Shortly, after carrying straight on at the 'crossroads', you will cross two small, low, banks – part of a medieval field system – before seeing yet another green track coming in from the left. This you should now join by going off to the right, ignoring a secondary (much narrower) green path that also goes off to the right at this same point. There are now excellent views of Dartmoor: from left to right, the tors on the skyline are Cox, Great Staple, Great Mis and North Hessary, with its radio mast, near Princetown.

Continue to follow this well-defined green track for approximately a quarter of a mile until arriving at a distinct 'Y' junction. From here, take the left-hand fork and walk downhill to a bridge, which was built over the now disused Plymouth to Tavistock railway line as a means of providing access for the movement of livestock between the lower part of the valley and the open moorland. On arriving at this bridge, proceed to the far side and then follow the fencing around to the left before walking roughly parallel to it for about 100 yards by means of a small path. This path, in turn, will then lead you through a gap in the fencing and on to the track-bed of the old railway line, which should now be followed by turning left and passing underneath the same bridge that you crossed only a few minutes earlier.

After a while, you will be confronted by the sight of a large iron gate, which is situated at the northern end of the large, brick-built, Magpie Viaduct. Just before reaching it, on the right-hand side, are the remains of a P.W. (Permanent Way) hut and a small path leading up into the woods. However, before joining this path it is well worth continuing the short distance towards the iron gate across the railway track-bed so that a closer view of the top of the viaduct may be obtained.

The small path leading up into the woods diverges after only 35 yards or so. Take the left-hand fork, which will lead you around the back of an old quarry, and then descend to the first of what appears to be two small streams. This, in fact, is water flowing out of an old adit, which can clearly be seen upon arriving at the water's edge and which is just one of several old adits associated with Wheal Franco Mine.

From here, simply follow the water downstream by means of another small path, passing underneath Magpie Viaduct and taking note of the numerous spoil heaps associated with Wheal Franco Mine as you proceed, and this will very soon lead you back to your starting point, the car park at Bedford Bridge.

❋❋❋❋❋

Appendix 1: Glossary of Mining Terms

Adit: a horizontal tunnel driven into the side of a hill for drainage purposes and access. Also occasionally used for bringing ore to the surface.

Black Tin: tin ore ready for smelting after being crushed and cleansed, normally containing 65% or less of metallic tin.

Buddle: a rectangular or circular pit used for concentrating crushed tin ore.

Burning House: an old term for the building where the ore was crushed or 'burnt' (see also Calciner).

Calciner: a furnace in which the ore was roasted, either to drive off unwanted constituents or to sublimate them for separate recovery, or to render the ore more amenable to subsequent processes.

Captain: the title given to the person in charge of the operations at the mine.

Dresser: the title given to the person in charge of the cleaning of the crushed ore.

Dump: a pile of waste material/rock from the mine.

Fathom: a unit of length equivalent to 6 feet (1.8 metres).

Flat rods: oscillating iron rods linked to form a single rod which was used to transfer power from a waterwheel or engine house to another location.

Launder: a wooden gutter for conveying water, usually to a wheel.

Leat: an open channel dug into the ground for the purposes of conveying water from a stream or river to a mine.

Lode: an area of mineralisation.

Ore (Copper or tin): a copper-bearing or tin-bearing mineral.

Shaft: a vertical or inclined tunnel used for mining purposes.

Wheelpit: a pit in which a waterwheel turns.

✷✷✷✷✷

Appendix 2: Useful Addresses

DARTMOOR NATIONAL PARK
AUTHORITY,

Parke,
Haytor Road,
Bovey Tracey,
Newton Abbot. TQ13 9JQ
Tel: 01626 832093

THE HIGH MOORLAND
VISITOR CENTRE,

Old Duchy Hotel,
Princetown,
Yelverton. PL20 6QF
Tel: 01822 890414

TAVISTOCK INFORMATION
CENTRE,

Town Hall Building,
Bedford Square,
Tavistock.
Tel: 01822 612938

DARTMOOR TINWORKING
RESEARCH GROUP,

Esmee Sykes,
3 Tappers Close,
Topsham,
Exeter.

PLYMOUTH MINERAL &
MINING CLUB,

Ken Roberts,
Uppershaugh Farmhouse,
Shaugh Prior,
Plymouth. PL7 5HA
Tel: 01752 839274

DARTMOOR PRESERVATION
ASSOCIATION,

Old Duchy Hotel,
Princetown,
Yelverton. PL20 6QF
Tel: 01822 890646

WEST DEVON RECORD
OFFICE,

Unit 3,
Clare Place,
Coxside,
Plymouth.
Tel: 01752 385940

YELVERTON & DISTRICT
LOCAL HISTORY SOCIETY,

20 Rolston Close,
Southway,
Plymouth,
PL6 6PE

❇❇❇❇❇

BIBLIOGRAPHY

Barclay, C. F. & others. (1918–40) *Reports of local mines*. Unpublished MSS.

Burt, R., Waite, P. and Burney, R. (1984) *Devon & Somerset Mines*. University of Exeter.

Dartmoor Safe Walks Team. (1988) *Dartmoor Walks for Children*. The College of St. Mark & St. John.

Dines, H. G. (1956) *The Metalliferous Mining Region of South-West England*. Mem. Geol. Survey. HMSO.

Greeves, T. (1986) *Tin Mines and Miners of Dartmoor: A Photographic Record*. Devon Books.

Hamilton-Jenkin, A. K. (1974) *Mines of Devon. Vol. 1: The Southern Area*. David & Charles.

Harris, H. (1993) *Industrial Archaeology of Dartmoor*. Peninsula Press.

Hemery, E. (1983) *High Dartmoor – Land and People*. Hale.

Horrabridge Pensioners Club. *The Village of Horrabridge on the edge of Dartmoor*.

Kingdom, A. R. (1990) *The Plymouth Tavistock and Launceston Railway*. ARK Publications.

Laxton, P. (1996) *An Account of the History of Grenofen Manor*. Yelverton & District Local History Society Newsletter, No. 13.

Lewis, W. J. *West of England Tin Mining*.

Mobbs, Miss A. M. (1980) *Horrabridge & District Part 2, Tin and Copper Mines of Horrabridge*. Privately published.

Northworthy, J. (Pseudonym of P. Rendell) (1991) *Walking in the Tavy & Tamar*. (An article in *Around Tavy & Tamar*).

Prince, Elizabeth. (1979) *Dartmoor National Park Walks 2. South West Dartmoor*. Devon County Council.

Rendell, P. (1986) *A Riverside Walk – from Magpie to Grenofen* (An article in *Tavistock Times*).

Rendell P. (1993) *Tavistock Countryside Walks*. West Devon Borough Council.

Richards, P. H. G. (1992) *Mines of Dartmoor and the Tamar Valley after 1913*. Northern Mine Research Society.

White's Directory (1850).

❋❋❋❋❋

THE AUTHOR

Paul Rendell was born in Plymouth in 1961 and became enthusiastic about Dartmoor, especially its industrial archaeology, from an early age, when he was taken there on numerous outings by his parents.

After leaving school, Paul trained as a chef and worked in a number of establishments within the Plymouth area, as well as a few on Dartmoor. Later he was Head Gardener at Devonport Dockyard for several years, but by then his explorations of Dartmoor had already helped provide him with a knowledge of the moor that only a few possess: this, combined with sheer dedication, led to him becoming a full-time professional guide, which, in turn, has enabled him to introduce many people to the delights of walking on Dartmoor and throughout the West Country.

A keen historian, Paul is also Vice Chairman and Secretary of the Yelverton & District Local History Society, gives illustrated talks and has already had various articles published, the first being about the River Walkham. In addition, as founder and editor of *The Dartmoor Newsletter*, he is frequently out and about gathering information on matters appertaining to Dartmoor, and in his spare time enjoys reading, collecting old picture-postcards, listening to music and exploring the countryside.

Paul Rendell